KU-288-615

Why Living Things Need...

Homes

Daniel Nunn

www.raintreepublishers.co.uk
Visit our website to find out
more information about
Raintree books.

To order:
☎ Phone 0845 6044371
🖷 Fax +44 (0) 1865 312263
📧 Email myorders@raintreepublishers.co.uk

Customers from outside the UK please telephone +44 1865 312262

Raintree is an imprint of Capstone Global Library Limited,
a company incorporated in England and Wales having
its registered office at 7 Pilgrim Street, London, EC4V 6LB
– Registered company number: 6695582

Text © Capstone Global Library Limited 2012
First published in hardback in 2012
The moral rights of the proprietor have been asserted.

All rights reserved. No part of this publication may be
reproduced in any form or by any means (including
photocopying or storing it in any medium by electronic
means and whether or not transiently or incidentally to
some other use of this publication) without the written
permission of the copyright owner, except in accordance
with the provisions of the Copyright, Designs and Patents Act
1988 or under the terms of a licence issued by the Copyright
Licensing Agency, Saffron House, 6–10 Kirby Street, London
EC1N 8TS (www.cla.co.uk). Applications for the copyright
owner's written permission should be addressed to the
publisher.

Edited by Dan Nunn, Rebecca Rissman, and Sian Smith
Designed by Joanna Hinton-Malivoire
Picture research by Ruth Blair
Production by Victoria Fitzgerald
Originated by Capstone Global Library Ltd
Printed and bound in China by Leo Paper Products Ltd

ISBN 978 1 4062 3373 5
15 14 13 12
10 9 8 7 6 5 4 3 2

British Library Cataloguing in Publication Data
Nunn, Daniel.
  Why living things need... homes.
  1. Dwellings–Juvenile literature. 2. Housing–Juvenile
literature. I. Title
  643-dc22

Acknowledgements
We would like to thank the following for permission to
reproduce photographs: Corbis pp.10 (© Lance Nelson/
Stock Photos), 11 (© Juice Images), 17 (© D. Robert & Lorri
Franz); Photolibrary pp.7 (Michael Krabs/Imagebroker), 8
(Eric Baccega/Age fotostock), 12 (Fritz Polking/Peter Arnold
Images), 20 (J-L. Klein & M-L. Hubert/Bios); Shutterstock pp.4
(© Gerald A. DeBoer), 5 (© dusan964), 5 (© Rob Marmion),
5 (© Kevin E. Beasley), 5 (© tomy), 6 (© Tony Campbell), 9
(© tfrisch99), 13 (© Noam Armonn), 14 (© Caitlin Mirra),
15 (© Groomee), 16 (© John Carnemolla), 18 (© Arno
van Dulmen), 19 (© Vishnevskiy Vasily), 21 (© Monkey
Business Images), 22 (© visceralimage), 22 (© jokter), 22 (©
Inhabitant), 23 (© Tony Campbell), 23 (© Vishnevskiy Vasily).

Front cover photograph of a puffin reproduced with
permission of Photolibrary (Fritz Polking/Peter Arnold
Images). Back cover photograph of a bird building a nest
reproduced with permission of Shutterstock (© tfrisch99).

We would like to thank Nancy Harris, Dee Reid, and Diana
Bentley for their assistance in the preparation of this book.

Every effort has been made to contact copyright holders
of material reproduced in this book. Any omissions will be
rectified in subsequent printings if notice is given to the
publisher.

Contents

What is a home?

beehive

bees

A home is a place where something lives.

There are different kinds of homes.

Living things and homes

People and other animals are
living things.

Living things need homes.

Some animals find homes.

This bear lives in a cave.

Some animals build homes.

This bird lives in a nest.

Some people build homes, too.

This person's home is on a boat.

Why do living things need homes?

Homes keep living things safe.

Homes keep living things safe from the weather.

Homes keep animals safe from other animals.

Homes keep animals warm and dry.

How do living things use homes?

Some living things sleep in their homes.

Foxes sleep in their homes.

Some living things eat in their homes.

Birds bring food to their nests.

Some living things care for their young in their homes.

People care for their young
in their homes.

Homes quiz

Which of these things does not need a home?

Answer on page 24

Picture glossary

living thing something that is alive, such as an animal or a plant

nest a home made by birds or other animals out of grass or twigs

Index

Answer to question on page 22
The pig and the eagle need homes.
The traffic lights do not need a home.

Notes for parents and teachers

Before reading

Talk about why people live in homes. For example, homes keep people warm and dry, homes give people a place to sleep, a place to eat their food, and somewhere to keep their belongings. Ask them if they can think of some homes that animals have. What does a bird make its home out of? Where do bees make their home? Where do rabbits make their homes?

After reading

• Demonstrate how to use an information book to discover some interesting facts about animal homes. Take one example of an animal home and draw a simple sketch of the home on paper. Add a caption and talk about the writing process as you write. Invite children to draw different homes, for example, a cave, a nest, a rabbit's burrow, or a fox's den. Help them to add simple captions, for example: A fox's home is called a den.

• Tell the children they are going to pretend to be different animals looking for their homes. For example, explain that they are going to be rabbits. They should bunny hop around until you say that they have found their home. Then they can pretend to crawl down the burrow and lie down to sleep. Repeat with ideas for an owl in its hole, a bee in its hive, a bear in its cave, a spider in its web, and a horse in its stable.